SO-CWS-751

Be the Best
NATURE EXPLORER

A Step-By-Step Guide
By Carey Huber

Troll Associates

Library of Congress Cataloging-in-Publication Data

Huber, Carey.
    Nature explorer: a step-by-step guide / by Carey Huber.
      p.   cm.—(Be the best!)
    Summary: Provides information on where and how to identify, track,
and collect the wonders of nature.
    ISBN 0-8167-1953-5 (lib. bdg.) ISBN 0-8167-1954-3 (pbk.)
    1. Nature study—Juvenile literature. [1. Nature study.]
I. Title. II. Series.
QH51.H87 1990
508—dc20   89-27391

Copyright © 1990 by Troll Associates, Mahwah, New Jersey

All rights reserved. No part of this book may be used or reproduced in any manner whatsoever without written permission from the publisher.

Printed in the United States of America.

10 9 8 7 6 5 4 3 2 1

Be the Best

NATURE EXPLORER

A Step-By-Step Guide

FOREWORD

by David Bates

Nature Exploring, A Step-by-Step Guide, is a terrific book for young explorers. It is easy to read, informative, and will capture your imagination.

Maybe a new John Muir or Aldo Leopold, both great nature explorers and champions of conservation, is out there among you right now. This book may inspire *you* in that direction, and it is my pleasure to recommend it.

Dand Bates

David Bates is a leading U.S. authority on nature exploring, backpacking, camping, and other outdoor activities. He has been certified as an outdoor leader by the Wilderness Education Association. David is also a member of the Association for Experiential Education and both treasurer and board member of the American Camping Association's Coronado section. His enjoyment of the outdoors includes mountain climbing, and he has climbed over 100 peaks, including 14,410-foot (4,392-meter) Mount Rainier in Washington.

Contents

1

Exploring Nature

The world of nature is a place of wonder. It's filled with many exciting things to do. You can hike through grassy meadows and dense woods, identifying the bark and leaves of interesting trees. You can enjoy splashing through brooks and streams as you hunt for frogs and crayfish. You can be thrilled at the sight of wild birds and forest animals. You can even start a collection of bird pictures, pine cones, or animal tracks. Those are just a few of the many things a nature explorer can do.

Best of all, you don't have to pack up a tent and spend weeks camping out in the Rocky Mountains to explore nature. The world of nature can be discovered outside your back door, in a garden, or in a nearby field, park, campground, or public hiking trail. The world of nature is all around you. It can be as small as a back yard garden or as vast as a nature preserve. All you have to do is know where and how to look for the wonders of nature. And that's what you will learn in this book.

The first and most important rule of being a nature explorer is to have respect for nature and its wonders. Never litter or alter a wildlife area. Leave nature areas the way you found them or cleaner. Watch and study animals. But try not to disturb them in their natural *habitats* (places where certain animals are usually found). And remember, nearly all wild creatures are not suitable as pets. Following those rules, you can not only explore nature but also help to preserve it for generations to come.

Hiking

Hiking is a great way to explore nature and to see the great outdoors up close. A hike can be a short day trip to a park, pond, or wooded area. Or it can be a longer trip to a campground, lake, or forest. The kind of nature hikes you will probably take will be short trips to nearby streams or wildlife areas. For those kinds of hikes, you do not need any special equipment.

However, if you plan to spend a day hiking a good distance, certain items can make your outing more comfortable and enjoyable. There are also standard hiking rules you should always follow—no matter where you go or how long you plan to be away.

One of the most important rules of hiking is to take an adult with you whenever possible. If an adult cannot go with you, always hike with a friend or a group of friends. *Never* hike alone!

Before you leave, always plan where you will hike. Do not wander about aimlessly. A hike should have a start, a destination, and a return trip or finish. For example, plan on starting from your home, hiking to a pond or hill, and then returning after a rest. You can even make a map of your hiking route.

If you are going on a hike with friends, tell an adult where you are going and how long you plan to be gone. If you do make a map of your hiking route (which is always a good idea), leave a copy behind so you can be found easily in an emergency. Always start your hike as early in the day as you can, and always build in enough time to return from your destination. That way, you can see more things and be able to return home well before dark. Also, *never* hike so far that you're exhausted before you can make it back.

HIKING EQUIPMENT

It's a good idea to bring along the following items so that you'll be comfortable on a long hike. But remember this: You must carry what you bring. Items that seem light at the start of a hike will seem heavier at the end.

Clothing What you wear for hiking depends on where you plan to go, what you plan to do, and what time of year it is. In summer, shorts are usually fine. But in areas with a lot of insects, and in fall and spring, long pants are best. It is also wise to bring along a cap to protect your head and an extra sweatshirt or jacket just in case the weather turns bad.

Footwear   Wool socks are good for hiking because they soak up moisture and let air get to your feet.

Sturdy, waterproof, well-padded, high-top boots are best on rocky, wooded, swampy, or uneven terrain. They'll keep pebbles, leaves, twigs, dirt, and moisture from getting inside. For casual hikes over familiar, easy terrain, sneakers are fine.

But in either case, if your boots or sneakers are brand new, be sure to break them in *before* wearing them on a hike. Otherwise, you'll get blisters on your feet.

Backpack   A backpack or a knapsack is practically a must for serious hiking. It lets you carry the things you'll need while leaving your arms free. But that does not mean you must spend a lot of money on a backpack. A canvas book bag from school can easily double as an inexpensive hiker's backpack.

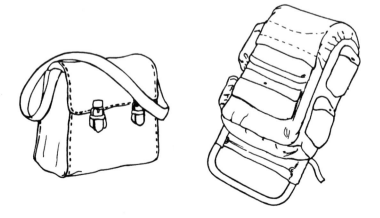

Canteen or Juice Packs   If you go on a hike and do not bring something to drink, you will be sorry. There are no soft-drink machines out in the woods. A canteen filled with water always comes in handy. If you do not have a canteen, pack some soft juice containers in your back-pack. And remember, when they are empty, do *not* throw them away in the woods. Carry them back home with you.

A Walking Stick   Any straight, sturdy stick that stands between waist and chest high will make a good walking stick. It will help you keep your balance and clear a path as you hike. A walking stick can also probe into spots where you might not want to put your hand (say, in a rock opening or murky pond). And it can also be used to ward off animals that come too close. If you find a walking stick you like, be sure to save it for future hikes.

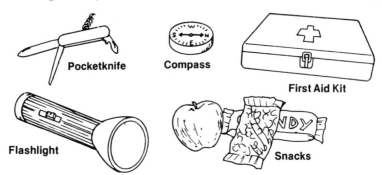

Pocketknife   Compass

First Aid Kit

Flashlight

Snacks

Other Items   You should also consider putting in your backpack a pocketknife, a flashlight, a map and compass, candy bars and fruit (for snacking), a first-aid kit, sun-screen, extra money, an identification card, and wooden matches. (Regular cardboard matches are usually no good after they get wet.)

3

Taking a Nature Walk

While taking a hike or nature walk, you can best appreciate nature by keeping your eyes and ears open and your mouth closed. Talking, especially loud talking or whistling, will scare away many of the birds and wild animals you hope to see. In the woods, silence really is golden. Being quiet also allows you to hear the sounds of the forest, such as birds singing and squirrels chattering.

As you move down a nature trail, walk slowly and step lightly. Branches that crack underfoot frighten game and alert animals to your presence. Any strange sound will cause an animal to hide or scurry away.

Moving slowly allows you to see things that might pass unnoticed at a quicker pace. Look for such animals as chipmunks, rabbits, and raccoons hiding along the trail or path. Check for animal tracks. Look for interesting plants, trees, and stones. Being a nature explorer means just that—exploring everything around you.

4

Exploring and Identifying Trees

Did you know there are thousands of different kinds of trees? That's why they're such common sights on nature walks. And how can you tell one tree from another? Well, there are several ways to identify trees.

Most conifers are softwoods. The name "conifer" comes from the fact that these trees have cones. Most conifers shed needles only a few at a time in fall, so they appear to stay ever green. That is why they are sometimes called "evergreens."

In contrast, hardwood trees have broad, flat leaves. When the weather turns cold in the fall, most hardwood trees begin to lose their leaves.

Why do conifers keep most of their needles while most hardwood trees lose their leaves in fall and winter? One main reason is that conifers have a thick, waxy covering on their needles. This prevents water in the leaves from *evaporating* (turning into vapor). The broad, flat leaves of the hardwood trees, however, usually do not have this outer protection. And so their water either evaporates or retreats back into the trees themselves. When that happens, the leaves of hardwood trees lose

TREE SHAPES

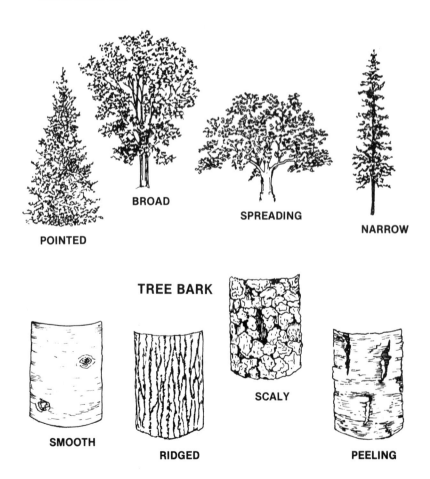

BROAD

SPREADING

NARROW

POINTED

TREE BARK

SCALY

SMOOTH

RIDGED

PEELING

their green coloring and turn into the fiery colors of autumn before finally shedding.

And how can you tell a hardwood tree from a softwood tree? You can feel the difference in the actual wood of the trees. The wood of hardwood trees is harder than the wood of softwood trees. That's how each got its name.

There are many kinds of hardwoods and softwoods, and there are several other ways to tell which tree is which. One way is the overall shape of the tree. A tree shape can be pointed, broad, spreading, or narrow. A tree's bark is also a good clue to its identity. There are four basic kinds of tree bark: smooth, ridged, plated or scaly, and peeling. Each tree also has its own unique leaf pattern.

What follows are more specific clues that can help you recognize different types of trees.

IDENTIFYING HARDWOODS

Here are some of the more common hardwood trees and how they can be identified.

Oak There are many different kinds of oak trees. Most are broad shaped and have a ridged bark. However, different oaks have different styles of leaves. The best and easiest way to identify an oak is by acorns. All oak trees produce acorns. If you see an acorn, it's from an oak tree. Some types of oaks are red oak, white oak, bur oak, pin oak, willow oak, and live oak.

ACORNS

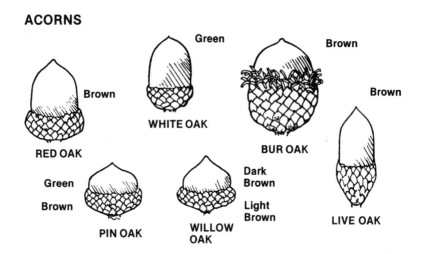

Maple   As with the oak, there are many kinds of maple trees. Each one has its own unique bark and leaf formation. However, like oaks, all maple trees have something in common. That something is the unique fruit all maples produce. Maples have winged fruit shaped like insects. Sometimes the seeds spin like tiny helicopter blades as they fall. Some types of maples are red maple, silver maple, sugar maple, and Norway maple.

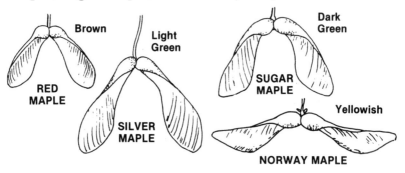

Shagbark Hickory   The shagbark hickory is easy to recognize. It has unique, saggy, peeling bark that seems to hang in strips. It also produces very hard-shelled nuts that squirrels love to eat.

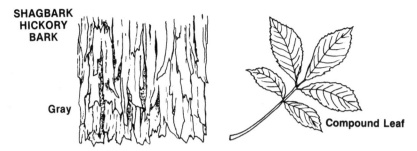

SHAGBARK HICKORY BARK

Gray

Compound Leaf

Sycamore   The sycamore is another tree easily recognized by its bark. Sycamore trees have peeling bark that can be flaked off in pieces. The bark is made up of mixed colors: gray, white, light green, and brown.

Sycamores also have unique seeds. They look like tiny, bumpy golf balls on a stem.

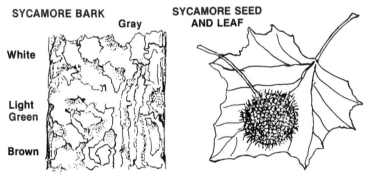

SYCAMORE BARK

Gray

White

Light Green

Brown

SYCAMORE SEED AND LEAF

Canoe Birch   The canoe birch can be easily identified by its strange-looking bark. The canoe birch has silvery-white peeling bark with brownish wrinkles that ring the trunk. The bark is waterproof, and it was once used by American Indians to build canoes. It can be peeled off the tree in strips.

The seeds of the birch are produced in long, fuzzy strings called *catkins.* Hanging from the birch's branches, catkins are shaped like cat's tails. Some people think they also look like very plump caterpillars.

19

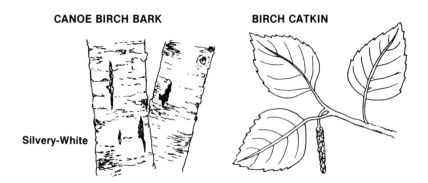

CANOE BIRCH BARK   **BIRCH CATKIN**

Silvery-White

Elm   The easiest way to identify an elm tree is by its overall shape. Elms have long trunks and wide, leafy domes. They kind of look like a big umbrella. The leaf of the elm is also easy to recognize. It is lopsided, and the pointed leaf has one side wider than the other. Elm bark looks like a network of ridges.

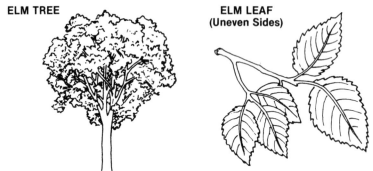

ELM TREE   **ELM LEAF**
(Uneven Sides)

White Ash   The white ash is a large spreading tree. Its wood is light and strong, and is often used to make baseball bats.

The bark of the white ash has deep, fine ridges. It also has pointed leaves that grow opposite each other in groups.

The easiest way to recognize a white ash is by its fruit. Like the maple, it has winged fruit. However, the fruit of the white ash has only one wing and forms in clusters.

WHITE ASH
Fruits And Leaves

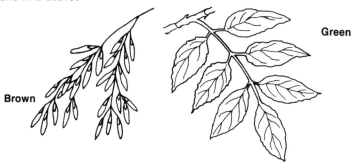

Green

Brown

Honey Locust   The honey locust tree has smooth bark and groups of small, fanlike leaves. This tree also has many clusters of long, sharp thorns that grow out of its trunk, branches, and limbs.

The seeds of the honey locust are enclosed in long, slender strips that are brownish purple. They almost look like dried-up leeches.

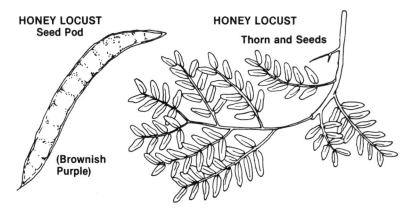

HONEY LOCUST
Seed Pod

HONEY LOCUST

Thorn and Seeds

(Brownish Purple)

IDENTIFYING EVERGREENS

Most conifers are also evergreens. They produce their seeds in cones, which consist of stiff, overlapping, woody scales. An example is the pine cone.

There are five general types of evergreen trees. They are pine, spruce, hemlock, cedar, and fir. Each type has several different varieties. And each variety has its own needle formation and cone shape.

Pine Pine needles can be very long or very short, depending on the type. They can also be formed in bundles of two or three.

Pine cones grow downward and can be large, medium, or small sized. The common white pine, for example, has a slightly curved cone.

Some other types of pine trees are the lodgepole pine, limber pine, Jeffrey pine, and loblolly pine.

PINE CONE TYPES

WHITE PINE CONE

Cone Has Scales That Stick Out

Light Brown

LODGEPOLE PINE CONE

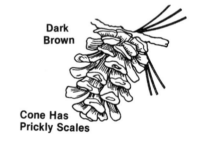

Dark Brown

Cone Has Prickly Scales

JEFFREY PINE CONE

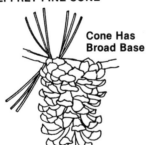

Cone Has Broad Base

LOBLOLLY PINE CONE

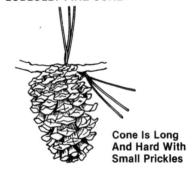

Cone Is Long And Hard With Small Prickles

Fir Fir trees have flat, soft, tightly grouped needles. The cones of the balsam fir grow up from the branches rather than hang down from them. Cones from the Douglas fir hang down from the branches but have hairlike bristles called *bracts* sticking out.

BALSAM FIR CONES   **DOUGLAS FIR CONE**

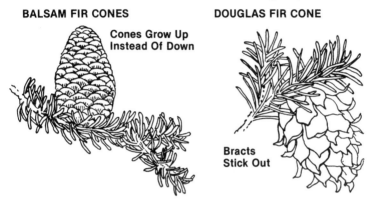

Cones Grow Up
Instead Of Down

Bracts
Stick Out

Hemlock Hemlock trees have small needles. The needles have two silver bands underneath, which make the hemlock easy to identify. Hemlock cones are very small.

HEMLOCK

Needles

Two Silver Bands
Underneath

Spruce As with pines, there are many kinds of spruce trees. Two kinds, Norway and blue spruce, have the longest cones of any conifers. They are also the most common types of spruce trees.

The wood from spruce trees is often used to make paper.

**Cone Is Long
And Has Tight
Scales**

Cedar   Cedar trees have extremely short, close-cropped, very dense needles. These needles are actually formed into flat sprays of leaves.

Cedar trees also have small, clustered cones.

CEDAR TREE
Needles and Cones

**Needles Are Short And Dense,
Forming Flat Sprays
Of Leaves**

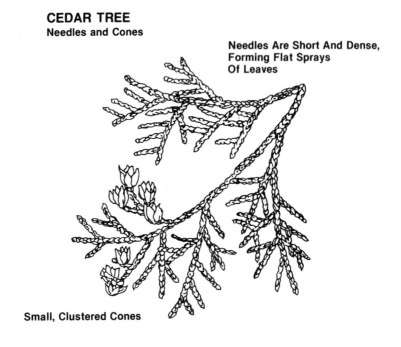

Small, Clustered Cones

Tree Fun

Now that you've learned how to identify some trees, here are some other ways you can have some tree fun.

CONE COLLECTING

Different conifers have different kinds of cones (see pages 21-24). You can collect these various cones and then glue them in a cardboard box. See how many different ones you can find. And make sure you identify and label each one.

BARK RUBBINGS

A bark rubbing is easy to make. Use a piece of strong but thin white or yellow paper. Press the paper against the bark of a tree trunk. With a soft lead pencil or a crayon, gently rub across the paper until the bark pattern appears on the paper. You can make a record of many different kinds of tree bark this way.

PRESSING LEAVES

Collecting leaves can be fun and informative. This is especially true in autumn, when the leaves of most hardwood trees are falling.

To press leaves, put a leaf between two sheets of soft, absorbent paper. (Newspaper is good for this.) Then put the sheets under a heavy book. And finally, put something heavy, such as a rock, on top of the book.

After a week or so, the leaf will dry out. You can then paste it in a notebook or scrapbook. Just remember to label your leaves.

Identifying
Dangerous Plants

While hiking or taking a nature walk in the woods, stay away from poison ivy, poison oak, and poison sumac. Touching any of these three plants could give you a painful, itchy rash.

POISON IVY

Poison ivy has three broad, oval-shaped leaves. The middle leaf is bigger than the other two. It grows on a creeping vine with hairy roots. It can grow up tree trunks or on the ground. In the fall, poison ivy leaves turn bright red, and the vine produces little hard berries that can be white, pale green, or cream colored.

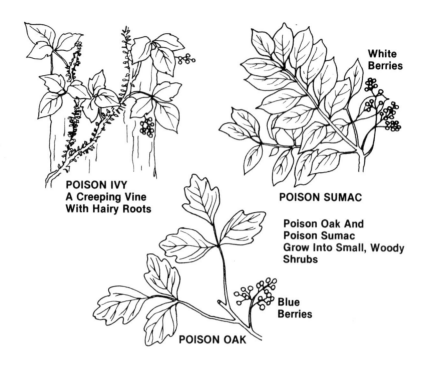

POISON IVY
A Creeping Vine
With Hairy Roots

White
Berries

POISON SUMAC

Poison Oak And
Poison Sumac
Grow Into Small, Woody
Shrubs

Blue
Berries

POISON OAK

POISON OAK

Poison oak is more like a twig than a vine. It grows in woods and fields. Poison oak has a thin, brown stem and leaves with rounded lobes. These leaves are usually clustered in groups of three. Poison oak also produces small, round, blue-colored berries.

POISON SUMAC

Like poison oak, poison sumac is more treelike than poison ivy. But the branches of poison sumac are thicker than those of poison oak. The slender, pointed leaves of poison sumac grow in groups—one on each side of the stem. Poison sumac produces white berries.

Bird Watching

Bird watching may sound dull and boring, but it really isn't. Finding and watching birds in the wild can be fun and fascinating.

While taking a nature walk through a meadow or forest, you can see many kinds of birds. Hawks glide above. Quail and pheasants scamper through the brush. And the treetops are often the homes of robins, thrushes, jays, and still other birds.

HOW TO BEGIN

Binoculars or field glasses make bird watching more enjoyable. They allow you to see birds up close. But binoculars are not a necessity. You can spot and watch birds with your naked eye as you walk along. While walking, check treetops, shrubs, bushes, and the ground for birds. Also keep your ears open for singing birds.

If you spot a bird, stop. Slowly approach the bird straight ahead for a better look. Birds are easily frightened by sideways movements. Approaching a bird head on will enable you to get fairly close to it.

Once you have a good view of the bird, stand still and observe its habits. What is it doing? Is it looking for food? Is it singing? What does its song sound like? That is the way you learn about birds. After watching the bird for a while, move on. And try not to scare the bird as you leave.

HOW TO IDENTIFY BIRDS

Color is one easy way to identify a bird. What is the bird's main color? Does it have other colors on its wings, head, throat, legs, and belly? Those are all clues to a bird's identity. And keep in mind that male birds are often more colorful than female birds.

Next, what is the size and shape of the bird? Is it bigger than a sparrow or a robin but smaller than a crow? You can use the sizes of these three common birds as standards for measuring new birds. (A sparrow is six inches long, a robin is ten inches long, and a crow is twenty inches long.)

The way a bird flies can also help you learn a bird's identity. Some birds glide or soar. Others bounce as they fly. Some move through the air in a straight line.

Finally, the sound a bird makes or its song is an excellent clue to the kind of bird it is.

BEST TIME TO SEE BIRDS

Almost all birds are active early in the morning and late in the afternoon. Those are the times birds feed, and you can see them moving around as they look for food. Bird watching is best at those peak hours.

GAME BIRDS

Carefully scan thick brush and tall grass as you move quietly through a field or meadow. You may see some of the following game birds. These are large birds sometimes hunted for food.

Ring-Necked Pheasant This bird has a long, pointed tail. It remains still when alerted to danger. The female is light brown with dark specks. The male is darker and more colorful, with an indigo head and a white ring around his neck.

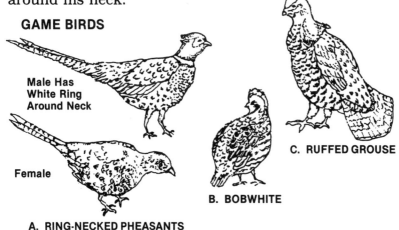

GAME BIRDS

Male Has White Ring Around Neck

Female

A. RING-NECKED PHEASANTS

B. BOBWHITE

C. RUFFED GROUSE

Bobwhite   Found in meadows and pastures, a bobwhite is brown and white with a white patch on its throat. Its call sounds like it is repeating its own name.

Ruffed Grouse   Smaller than a pheasant, this bird has a fantail and hides in tall grass. The ruffed grouse is brown and white, with bands of those colors across its belly.

SONGBIRDS

Check trees and bushes for glimpses of these common birds. They all have pleasant calls or songs.

Blue Jay   This bird has a white belly and face. Its back and tail are light blue with black stripes. The blue jay likes oak trees because acorns are one of its favorite foods.

Cardinal   The male bird is bright red from beak to tail. It has a pointy crest and a splash of black around its eyes. The female cardinal is light brown with rusty-red wings, tail, and crest. Cardinals make a high-pitched chirping sound.

Goldfinch   This tiny bird has black-and-white wings and tail. The rest of its body is bright yellow. The male has a patch of black on the top of its head.

Song Sparrow   The size of a finch, the little song sparrow is brown, black, and grayish white. It has a grayish belly covered with broken, brownish-black stripes.

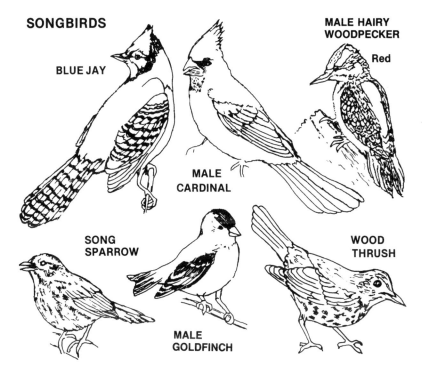

SONGBIRDS

BLUE JAY

MALE CARDINAL

MALE HAIRY WOODPECKER

Red

SONG SPARROW

MALE GOLDFINCH

WOOD THRUSH

Hairy Woodpecker This bird has a white belly and light, black-and-white striped wings. The male has a dab of red behind its black-and-white striped head.

Wood Thrush The back, wings, and tail of a wood thrush are brown. But its belly is white, with large brown specks on it.

WATER BIRDS

These are swimming or wading birds usually found on open water. Among the most common water birds are ducks and geese. They have short, webbed feet and can swim easily. They use their bills to sift the water for tiny insects and plants. Some ducks even dive briefly for their food.

Blue-Winged Teal Duck   This bird is common to most open-water areas. It is brown, gray, white, and blue. The male has a blue head, with a streak of white around the bill and eyes.

WATER BIRDS

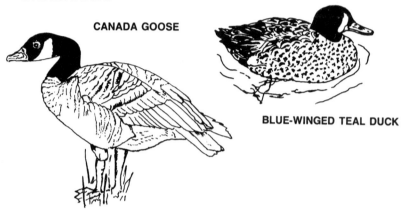

CANADA GOOSE

BLUE-WINGED TEAL DUCK

Canada Goose   A large water bird, the Canada goose has a grayish belly and brown wings. It has a long black neck, with a dab of white under its throat and behind its eyes. In fall and spring, flocks of Canada geese migrate, flying in a V formation.

SOME OTHER BIRDS

The following birds are just a few of the many thousands of other birds that inhabit the earth.

Hawk   A bird of prey, the hawk has a short, hooked bill for tearing flesh and strong claws for grasping and killing. It usually hunts during the day, and it hunts alone. Among the more common hawks are the broad-winged hawk and the red-tailed hawk. They can often be seen gliding high above fields and meadows, searching for small animals and other birds to kill.

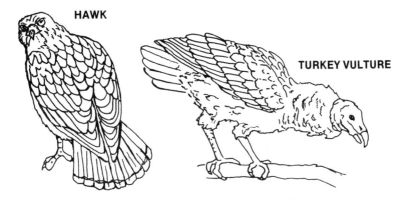

Turkey Vulture   This is a large, black-and-brown bird with a small red head. It has a huge wingspan (length from tip to tip when in flight), and soars in wide circles, looking for dead birds and animals. Sometimes you can see three or four turkey vultures together in the sky.

KEEPING A BIRD LIST

Beginning bird watchers can add to the fun of sighting wild birds by keeping a list of the birds they see. Take a small note pad and pencil with you on nature hikes. When you spot a bird, jot down the name of the bird, what it is doing, and when and where you saw it. If you do not know the name of the bird, write down the features that stand out. They will help you identify it later.

When your walk or hike is over, write your bird information in a notebook. It will be your permanent record and checklist. You can even sketch pictures of birds you see if you like to draw.

BIRD BOOKS

Books that contain full-color photos and illustrations of birds in your state can be found in your local library. Such a book can help you identify and learn more about birds native to your area. It may even tell you where you can sight interesting birds.

FEATHER COLLECTING

Sometimes, especially during spring, you can find many bird feathers lying on the ground or stuck in bushes. If you enjoy collecting things, such as cones or leaves, you may also enjoy collecting bird feathers. Just tape the feathers you find to pages in a notebook. Most birds can be identified by a single feather. If you're unsure of one, look it up in a bird book that has full-color photos and illustrations.

Adventures
Around Water

A freshwater brook, creek, stream, or shallow pond is a great place to explore nature. You may see a whole range of different plants, animals, fish, and birds.

But you must be very careful when you're near water. Never try to wade in fast-moving water or water above your knees, and don't enter water that is so murky you cannot see the bottom. Also, never venture into water if you do not know how deep it is. Even in shallow water, there is always the danger of drowning. So be careful when you step on slippery stones or moss-covered rocks. A wise nature explorer is always careful and never takes foolish chances.

CRAYFISH

Crayfish are small crustaceans (water creatures that usually have some kind of shell) that look like tiny lobsters. They live in brooks, creeks, and the shallow parts of streams, rivers, and ponds. Crayfish can be as tiny as the tip of your pinky or as large as your biggest finger. Finding and catching crayfish can be lots of fun.

To catch crayfish, you can use a cup, a bucket, an old can, or just your hand. Crayfish have claws resembling pincers, but they cannot squeeze your skin hard enough to hurt. So do not be afraid to handle them.

Crayfish like to hide under rocks in the water. Walk along the stream slowly, turning over stones in the water as you do. Wait for the rising cloud of mud to clear. Look in the water where you turned over the stone. You may see a crayfish crawling along the bottom.

Crayfish swim backward very quickly in spurts. To catch one, hold a cup, can, or your hand behind the crayfish's tail. Put your other hand in the water, moving it toward the front of the crayfish. The crayfish will be frightened and swim backward into the cup or can. Quickly lift up the cup to prevent it from swimming out.

Tiny Crayfish Like To Hide Under Rocks
In Brooks And Streams

38

To hold a crayfish, gently grab it from the back just above its tail. Hold it lightly between your thumb and first finger.

Captured crayfish can be kept in a bucket or pail of creek water as you continue to hunt for more. However, crayfish are cannibals. The big ones may try to eat the little ones, and they may fight in the pail. But usually they just try to avoid each other.

When you tire of crayfish hunting, release the ones you've caught back into the brook. Otherwise, you could disturb the natural order of things. For example, cranes, storks, raccoons, and otters feed on crayfish. Reducing the number of crayfish, then, could reduce the food supply for those creatures.

SNAILS

Most places that have crayfish will also have snails (creatures that usually have spirally coiled shells). Snails are scavengers. They eat things left behind by other water dwellers.

KINDS OF FRESHWATER SNAILS

FRESHWATER PERIWINKLE

GREAT RAMSHORN

GREAT POND SNAIL

JENKIN'S SPIRE SNAIL

There are many kinds of snails in brooks and ponds. The great ramshorn, great pond snail, freshwater periwinkle, and Jenkin's spire snail are all common types. Each one has a differently shaped shell.

You can pick up snails by their shells and collect them. Fill a container such as a glass tank or jar with brook water, some water plants, stones, and a little gravel. Then put the snails you catch in the container.

SALAMANDERS

Salamanders (like frogs and toads discussed next) are amphibians. That means they can live on land *and* in water. Usually, they're found in ponds, streams, and other wet areas.

Salamanders are tailed amphibians. They are generally three to eight inches long from their snout to the tip of their tail. They eat worms, live insects, and insect eggs.

KINDS OF SALAMANDERS

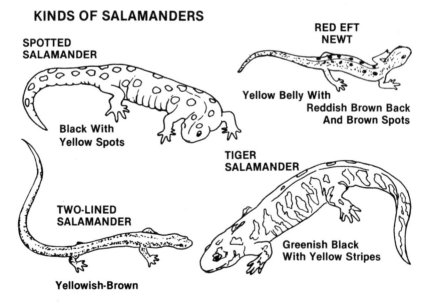

RED EFT NEWT

SPOTTED SALAMANDER

Black With Yellow Spots

Yellow Belly With Reddish Brown Back And Brown Spots

TIGER SALAMANDER

TWO-LINED SALAMANDER

Greenish Black With Yellow Stripes

Yellowish-Brown

Many salamanders spend their lives in water. Others live near water or in moist places, and then return to the water only to mate or lay eggs.

Salamanders can be found under rocks in streams, near water plants, or in muddy bottoms. They can also be found around and in most rotting material such as piles of wet leaves and old, fallen timber.

Although they feel a bit slimy, salamanders are harmless and can be caught in your bare hand. Most make good pets when kept in containers that re-create as much of their natural home as possible. That means small logs, marsh or water plants, stones or small rocks, and plenty of water to swim in and sand to rest on. Some common types of salamanders are the spotted salamander, the tiger salamander, newts (which are brightly colored salamanders), and the two-lined salamander.

FROGS AND TOADS

Frogs and toads are probably the best-known amphibians. They are found in or around most wet areas. Most kinds of frogs and toads spend at least part of their lives in water. Frogs remain near water once they grow up. Toads, however, move away and go off to live on dry land.

Frogs and toads lay jelly-covered eggs in clumps or long strings in still or slow-moving water. You can easily spot the eggs in quiet brooks and streams.

The eggs hatch into tadpoles (baby frogs and toads). The tadpoles live in the water and breathe through gills. They eat very tiny water plants.

FROG'S LIFE CYCLE

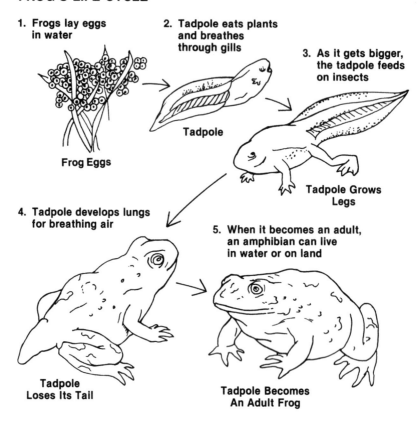

1. Frogs lay eggs in water

2. Tadpole eats plants and breathes through gills

3. As it gets bigger, the tadpole feeds on insects

Tadpole

Frog Eggs

Tadpole Grows Legs

4. Tadpole develops lungs for breathing air

5. When it becomes an adult, an amphibian can live in water or on land

Tadpole Loses Its Tail

Tadpole Becomes An Adult Frog

As they get older, the tadpoles grow legs and lose their tails. They also develop lungs for breathing air. Soon the tadpoles begin to feed on insects. And before long, they leave their watery home as adult frogs and toads.

In cold places, frogs and toads hibernate, or sleep through the winter, in underground burrows or in mud at the bottom of ponds.

Where to Look Tadpoles can be found swimming around in pools of water. There are usually several tadpoles in one place. They swim forward in short spurts. Use a can, bucket, or cup if you want to catch them.

Frogs can be found by walking along the edges of brooks, ponds, and creeks. Rustle the grass along the edges of the bank with a stick or the tip of your foot. That will cause the frogs to leap into the water. Watch where they jump and hide. Use a net, bucket, or your hands to catch frogs.

Tadpole Farm   You can watch tadpoles grow into frogs right before your eyes. First, collect some frog eggs from a brook or pond. Then put them in a fish tank or jar filled with pond water. Include some water plants and weeds from the pond in the tank. The young tadpoles will need to eat the water plants later.

After a while, the eggs will hatch into tiny tadpoles. As the tadpoles get older, they will need meat to eat. (In the wild, they would be eating insects.) To feed them, tie small chunks of raw meat to strings. Dip the meat in the water so it hangs above the bottom. The tadpoles will nibble at the meat.

TADPOLE–FROG TANK

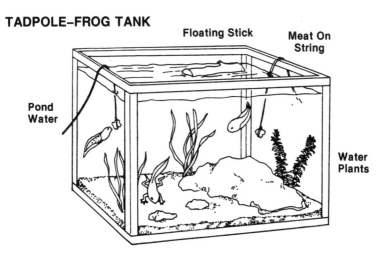

Floating Stick

Meat On String

Pond Water

Water Plants

As the tadpoles turn into frogs, they will need a way to get out of the water. Put a floating piece of wood in the jar for the young frogs to climb onto. Once the tadpoles lose their tails, release them back into the wild.

If you want to keep a frog or toad as a pet, empty a fish tank of water and make a screen lid for it (so the frog can't jump out). Place a dish of water in the tank and fill the bottom of the tank around the dish with dirt or sand. Put in some rocks, twigs, and plants. That will make a happy home for your pet frog or toad. Toads and frogs eat worms and all kinds of insects.

TURTLES

Like snakes, lizards, and crocodiles, turtles are *reptiles*. These are egg-laying, cold-blooded animals whose body temperature stays about the same as their surroundings. In cold weather, they have a hard time keeping warm and active. That's why turtles, like all reptiles, cannot live in areas that are cold year-round. (Human beings are warm-blooded and so can live in cold climates throughout the year.)

Turtles are the only reptiles with shells. Most of them can pull their head, legs, and tail inside their shells as protection against enemies. Turtles live in deserts, forests, lakes, marshes, prairies, meadows, and the sea. Some are dangerous, but most are harmless.

Finding land-dwelling turtles is usually a matter of luck. They like moist, open woods or swamps. Water turtles are easier to see. If you walk quietly and look carefully along a wide stream, river, or pond, you will probably see some turtles. Turtles like to climb up on rocks, floating logs, and dense sea plants to sun themselves.

TURTLE SUNNING ITSELF

Turtles do not have teeth, but they do have horny bills that can tear up plant and animal food. Turtles eat worms, bugs, fish, shellfish, grubs, and plants.

There are many kinds of turtles. But some of the most common ones in the United States are the:

Painted Turtle This turtle has a broad, dark, smooth-edged flat shell. The shell is usually black or very dark green. The edges of the shell are streaked with thin red lines. The turtle's head and neck are streaked with yellow and red stripes.

Painted turtles often cluster in groups on rocks or logs to sun themselves. They are shy and not easily captured.

Soft-Shelled Turtle Despite its name, this turtle really has a hard shell. Its black, shiny shell is smooth with soft edges. It has a long neck, a sharp beak, and a bad temper. It will bite if you try to capture it.

Common Snapper Big, mean, and dangerous, this turtle has a long, pointy tail and a long, thick neck. Snappers are green and have small shells. These turtles can't pull their head, legs, and tail inside their shells. That's why they rely on their strong, sharp-edged jaws for defense. Their claws are also very sharp. Stay far away from these grouchy old turtles.

COMMON SNAPPER

Box Turtle Slow-moving and mild-mannered, box turtles are found in open woods, fields, and swamps. They are brown and black, with splashes of yellow on their heads and shells. When frightened, box turtles pull their head and legs way inside their shells.

BOX TURTLE

Watching
Forest Animals

Seeing animals in the wild, especially while taking a hike or nature walk, is often a matter of luck. More often than not, animals hear or smell people approaching long before they arrive. That's how the animals are often alerted to possible danger, giving them enough time to run off and hide.

If you are very quiet and extremely watchful, however, you may have the good luck to surprise a deer, raccoon, chipmunk, or other forest animal. The best times to see wild animals are early in the morning, late in the afternoon, or after the sun sets.

Many forest animals, such as the opossum and owl, are *nocturnal*. That means they only come out after dark. Seeing nocturnal animals is very difficult if you are not camping out. And it is *not* a good idea to be exploring nature after dark. Instead, you should be home by then or at least not far from it when the sun sets. Remember, it is very easy to lose your way in the dark.

Also, keep in mind that most of the animals you'll meet in the woods are wild. Some, like the box turtle, pose no real threat to you. But others can. And even supposedly "friendly" animals, such as rabbits and squirrels, can carry disease. As a general rule, *avoid* trying to touch, catch, or trap wild animals in the forest.

FINDING OR BUILDING A BLIND

A very good way to see and watch wild animals and birds is from a *blind.* This is simply a hiding place for people that blends in with a forest or meadow. A blind can be natural or it can be made.

For natural blinds, sit near some bushes, behind a fallen tree, or in tall grass. That will hide you from the animals' sight.

To make a blind quickly, pile up branches, pieces of brush, or long weeds. Good places to build blinds are near streams and watering places, and at the edges of corn fields and meadows where animals such as deer come to graze.

WILD ANIMALS YOU MAY SEE

With or without the help of a blind, these are some of the wild animals you may see on an ordinary nature hike:

Gray Squirrel A rodent like the mouse, rat, chipmunk, and beaver, this animal is a common sight in and around large old trees. The gray squirrel is gray with a white belly and a bushy, white-tipped tail. This busy forest animal lives in tree holes or makes nests out of piles of leaves and branches. When angry or afraid, the gray squirrel chatters noisily and flicks its tail back and forth excitedly.

Cottontail Rabbit Long-eared and short-tailed, the cottontail rabbit is brown, gray, and white. Cottontails are found in fields and meadows where they like to burrow. They also like to hide around fallen trees, fences, and berry bushes. A cottontail will sit very quietly and still, hoping you will pass it by. So keep your eyes open for it.

COTTONTAIL RABBIT

GRAY SQUIRREL

Field Mouse This is a tiny, fluffy rodent with small ears and a short tail. Field mice are gray and white. They are always scampering around fields and meadows where they nibble on crops.

Chipmunk This rodent is a colorful and cute little forest animal. Some chipmunks live in trees; others live in holes in the ground. Some have long tails; others have short tails. Chipmunks are gray or brown, with black and tan stripes on their sides. These animals look and act much like their larger cousins, the squirrels.

Muskrat A fat, furry, blackish-gray animal, the muskrat looks like a small beaver. However, muskrats have rat-like tails rather than flat ones. Muskrats are found near swamps, ponds, lakes, or slow-moving brooks and streams. They feed on water plants, snails, and small fish.

MUSKRAT

CHIPMUNK

FIELD MOUSE

Raccoon This animal likes to be around water. A raccoon is gray, black, or brown. It has splashes of black around its eyes that make it look like it is wearing a mask. The raccoon also has a bushy, black-ringed tail.

RACCOON

White-Tailed Deer This North American deer is light brown and white with dark spots when it's born. Young deer are called *fawns*. When the fawns grow up, their color changes to all gray or light reddish-brown. A female deer is called a *doe*. A male deer is called a *buck*. Bucks grow large antlers made of bone that they shed every spring. The older a buck is, the more points (sharp, branchlike ends) it will have on its antlers. Deer stay hidden in the woods during most of the day. But they come out into open fields to graze early in the morning and late in the afternoon.

WHITE-TAILED DEER

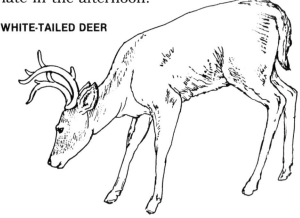

Tracking
Forest Animals

Many forest animals are hard to see. Some come out only at night. But all forest animals leave something behind when they wander around hunting for food— tracks. And a nature explorer can learn to identify them.

To find animal tracks, look around muddy creek or stream beds. Flat, dusty areas without grass also hold tracks well. Of course, tracks can also be found in winter snow. Another good time to look for animal tracks is shortly after a rain when the ground is still wet.

DEER TRACKS

Deer tracks are very easy to recognize. Deer have split hooves, with two toes on each foot. The front of a deer's toe is pointed. The back is rounded.

When a deer walks, it leaves two side-by-side toe tracks for each foot. The pointed ends show you the direction in which the deer went. If the toes are close together, then the deer was walking. If the toes are far apart, then the deer was running.

RABBIT TRACKS

A rabbit leaves two sets of tracks that look different. That is because a rabbit's back feet are larger than its front feet. The rabbit's rear feet leave long, boatlike tracks, and the front feet leave small, more rounded tracks.

The tracks of the back feet always appear in a side-by-side position. The reason is rabbits hop, bringing both of their back feet forward at the same time. The front feet, however, do not touch the ground side by side. One is a little in front of the other. Also, after a hop the back feet are planted ahead of the front feet.

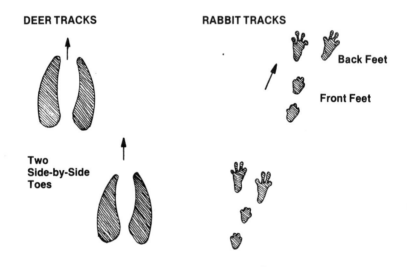

DEER TRACKS

Two Side-by-Side Toes

RABBIT TRACKS

Back Feet

Front Feet

SQUIRREL TRACKS

Squirrels hop when they are on the ground, and their tracks have tiny toes showing. The front feet have four toes each. The larger back feet have five toes each. Both the front and back tracks of a squirrel are paired side by side.

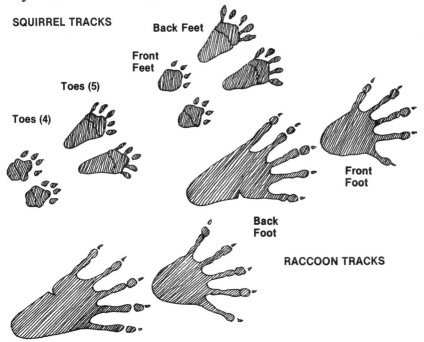

SQUIRREL TRACKS

Back Feet

Front Feet

Toes (5)

Toes (4)

Front Foot

Back Foot

RACCOON TRACKS

RACCOON TRACKS

Raccoon tracks look a little like the handprints and footprints of a human baby. Raccoons leave fat, rounded prints with five toes each on the front and back feet.

MUSKRAT TRACKS

Muskrats also have five toes on each foot. However, their front feet are much smaller than their back feet.

The tracks left by muskrats appear with the left front foot slightly ahead of the left rear foot and the right front foot slightly ahead of the right rear foot. Between these left and right tracks is a long straight line made by the muskrat's heavy tail.

OPOSSUM TRACKS

The opossum has five toes on each foot. However, the opossum's back foot has a huge, unclawed toe that juts out to the side. That makes opossum tracks easy to recognize.

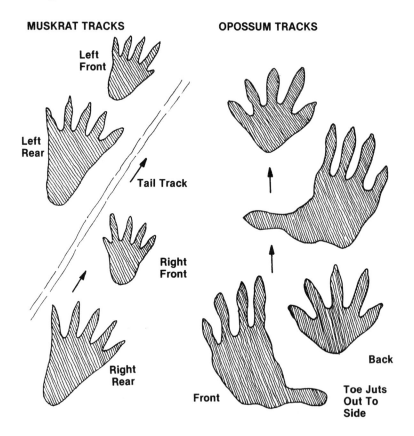

MUSKRAT TRACKS

Left Front

Left Rear

Tail Track

Right Front

Right Rear

OPOSSUM TRACKS

Front

Back

Toe Juts Out To Side

WEASEL TRACKS

The weasel has four toes and long, sharp claws on each foot. The back feet are slightly larger than the front feet.

SKUNK TRACKS

A skunk walks flat-footed. It has five toes on each foot. The tracks of its hind, or back, feet look somewhat like the tracks of human feet. The tracks of a skunk's front feet are much smaller than its back feet.

WEASEL TRACKS   **SKUNK TRACKS**

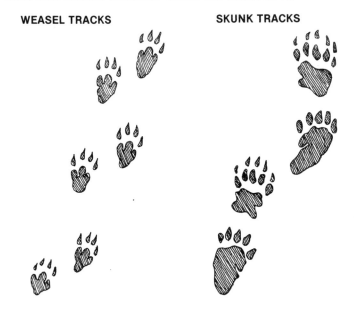

ORDINARY CAT TRACKS

The tracks left by an ordinary house cat show a triangular pad in the middle of each track and four toes. Cat tracks never show claw marks on the toes because cat's claws stay in when unused.

As a cat walks, it places its back foot almost right on top of the track made by its front foot on the same side.

ORDINARY DOG TRACKS

The tracks left by ordinary dogs resemble cat tracks. A dog has a triangle-shaped middle pad and four toes on each foot. The claws on a dog's toes usually show up in its tracks.

As a dog walks, it puts its back foot just ahead of the track left by its front foot on the same side.

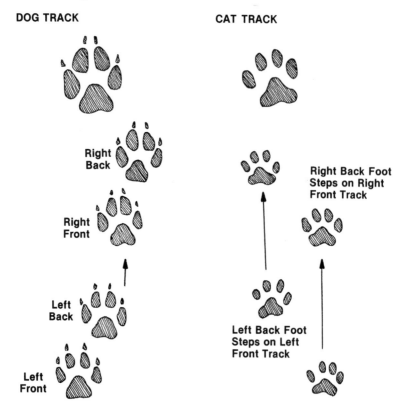

DOG TRACK

CAT TRACK

Right
Back

Right
Front

Left
Back

Left
Front

Right Back Foot
Steps on Right
Front Track

Left Back Foot
Steps on Left
Front Track

11

Having Fun
With Tracks

There are several ways you can have fun collecting tracks. You can take pictures of wild animal tracks with a camera and make a photo album of your finds. You can also draw sketches of the tracks you see, identify and label the drawings, and keep them in a notebook. You can even make cutouts from construction paper of your sketches.

But probably the most fun way to collect animal tracks is to make plaster molds of them. To do that, you will need to buy a bag of ordinary plaster of Paris. You can buy this at an art or hardware store. You will also need water, buckets to mix the plaster, and something to stir the mixture with. And finally, you will need long strips of sturdy paper, cut about one inch wide, and some paper clips.

After you find some animal tracks in mud or dirt, wrap a strip of paper around a track, forming a ring around it. Secure the strip into a ring by using a paper clip.

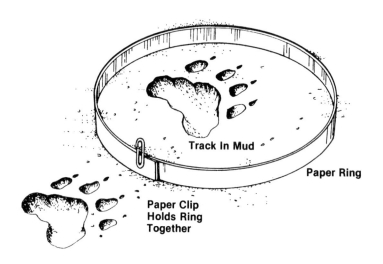

Track In Mud

Paper Ring

Paper Clip
Holds Ring
Together

Next, mix the plaster and water according to the directions on the package. Stir the mixture so it is not lumpy. You want it to run smoothly out of the container when you pour it.

Bucket And Water
For Mixing Plaster

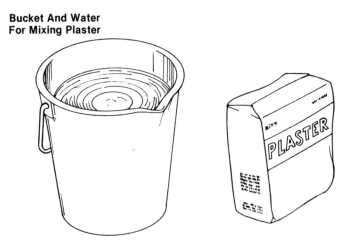

PLASTER

Pour the plaster into the track, filling up the ring of paper. Wait fifteen to twenty minutes for the plaster to dry. After it dries, cut off the paper ring with a knife. Lift up the plaster mold and brush off the dirt. You should have a perfect track cast in plaster.

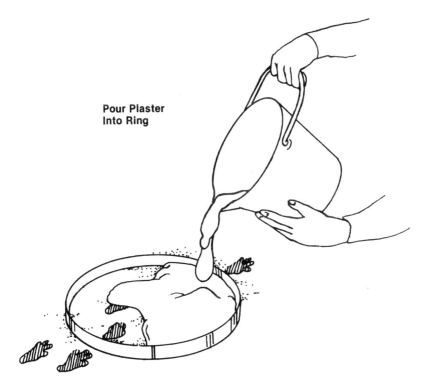

Pour Plaster Into Ring

You can also make plaster track casts in snow. But casting in snow does not always work, since snow and wet plaster can mingle. So don't be disappointed if your cast crumbles.

Nature—
A Great Treasure

Do you know what the most dangerous creatures in nature are? The answer is people. That's because people can either save or destroy wildlife areas and all living things in them. A carelessly thrown match can start a forest fire. Pollution in streams can kill fish and water-fowl. Unlawful hunting can drastically reduce the animal population of an area.

It's up to *all* nature explorers, young and old, to help preserve wildlife and wildlife areas. Forests, marshlands, deserts, mountains, and rivers should be treated with care. Leave them as you found them—wild and un-spoiled. That way, the person who comes after you will get the same chance to enjoy nature that you had.

Happy exploring!

INDEX